LOTUSLAND

LOTUSLAND
Eccentric Garden Paradise

PHOTOGRAPHY BY LISA ROMEREIN

RIZZOLI
NEW YORK

New York · Paris · London · Milan

CONTENTS

Many special plants have been selected to be named in homage to Lotusland and Madame Ganna Walska, including *Nymphaea* 'Madame Ganna Walska'. **PREVIOUS SPREAD**: The Fern Garden.

FOREWORD

Madame Ganna Walska, an international beauty who loved costumes and jewelry, was an aspiring opera singer whose lasting legacy turned out to be not on the stage, but in the soil. Her singing career over at the age of 54 and about to embark on what was to be an ill-fated sixth and final marriage, in 1941 she purchased, at her yogi fiancé's urging, a 37-acre estate in Santa Barbara, California, ostensibly for his use as a spiritual retreat. By 1946, however, the marriage had ended, and she wound up with the estate, dedicating the rest of her life to creating the garden that became Ganna Walska Lotusland. In 1958 she presciently established the foundation that would succeed her, and after she died in 1984, the garden began operation as a botanic garden, opening to the public in 1993.

I have been privileged to have been one of the many trustees and supporters who have contributed to the welfare of this remarkable garden and the growth of its horticultural programs. To experience Lotusland is to appreciate the idiosyncratic character of its creator. Her uniquely individual stamp is still very apparent, yet the garden that survives her has evolved and grown, as gardens do, and acquired a more complex identity. Even those of us familiar with it still struggle to define what makes it so magical. Perhaps its refusal to be easily categorized is part of the mystery.

As an architect who loves gardens, it is easier to understand gardens that have a clear geometric structure. It has been said that the definition of a garden is organized or controlled nature. Humans seem to be the only species not content to leave nature alone. From small vegetable plots to larger formal parterre gardens to vast agricultural orchards and fields, all are consciously arranged environments. The most extreme examples of this are perhaps the Renaissance and later classical gardens of Europe, where the geometry and axial organization often emanate from and relate to the villas and architecture to which they belong. The seventeenth-century gardens of Versailles are perhaps among the more famous examples of controlled nature.

Some gardens, exemplified by the eighteenth-century English landscapes designed by Capability Brown and Humphry Repton, pretend toward a more natural effect apparently untouched by human intervention. These too, however, are actually very self-consciously controlled re-compositions of nature, intentionally recreating idealized natural scenes on a grand scale. Trees, lakes, and terrain were often moved at great expense to make them.

There are a few gardens from more recent times, however, that defy traditional order and logic. They too have been consciously made, but over time and without a preconceived master plan. The Garden of Ninfa in Latina, Italy, or Little Sparta near Edinburgh, Scotland, come to mind. They have been inspired by instinct and appetite rather than planned logic, usually by an individual or family, and their development has been less predictable and more whimsical, often influenced by vicissitudes of mood and local circumstance.

I believe Lotusland, as conceived (rather than preconceived) by Ganna Walska, is among these rarer unstructured garden types. There was no master plan, its arrangement is not so easily understood, and it was character driven, in this case by her insatiable attraction to particular plants and her desire to create specific individual and often unrelated gardens within the larger garden. When she fell in love with something, a particular plant or garden ornament, she could not settle for just one or even a few but had to have a plethora. Hers was obsessive botanical collecting, often at a very ambitious scale, and the exuberance of the collections are a unique aspect of Lotusland's appeal.

As it has evolved as a nonprofit public garden over the last few decades since Ganna Walska's death, there has been a concerted effort toward sustainable horticultural practices and developing a sustainable business model. The botanical collections have grown and aged, however, without losing their powerful and sometimes exotic identities. There are some new additions, like the Dunlap Cactus Garden, and others have been expanded or refreshed, but the whimsy and character that were the inspiration for the original garden survive and assure Lotusland a special status as one of the most remarkable and magical places in the world.

The publication of this long-awaited book is finally an opportunity to share this unique garden with a wider audience. In person there is no mistaking the garden's appeal. In any publication it would be challenging to convey its eccentric qualities, but Lisa Romerein's photographs illuminate both the impressive scale of the collections as well as their poignant details, enticing those of us already familiar with the garden to look closer, and inviting those who have never had the chance to experience it to visit. To have been voted, as it recently was, one of the 10 best gardens in the world and among the top 100 to see before dying is an honor that might have made Madame Walska grin with delight. —*Marc Appleton*

PAGE 6: Succulents growing along the stone wall surrounding the sandy "beach" include *Cotyledon orbiculata*. OPPOSITE: *Dudleya brittonii* succulents are native to Baja California and have rosettes covered in chalky powder. They can reach eighteen inches in width.

INTRODUCTION

Ganna Walska Lotusland, a thirty-seven-acre oasis located in Montecito, California, is considered to be among the most significant botanic gardens in the world. Home to more than 3,400 types of plants, including at least 35,000 specimens, it is recognized not just for the breadth and diversity of its collections, but for the extraordinary design sensibility informing the many one-of-a-kind individual gardens that comprise its cohesive, harmonious, magical whole.

As delightfully pleasing as its aesthetic and sensory qualities are, Lotusland is also an important center for plant research and conservation. A leader in the field of sustainable horticulture, it was among the very first botanic gardens in the United States to employ environmentally responsible gardening practices. Innovative approaches utilize organic materials, some harvested from the garden itself, to create healthier plants rather than chemical interventions for pest and pathogen control, which can be toxic and degrade biological systems. Through such efforts, which also include serving as a leader to determine and teach others about best practices in the development of disease-suppressant soil, the garden has been able to create not only a stronger ecosystem overall, but also conserve natural resources.

The garden is a partner to many national and international organizations charged with conserving numerous species of plants from around the world that are threatened by extinction. Indeed, many of the plants cared for at Lotusland are threatened and are restricted from wild collection and international trade. The garden's assemblage of cycads is considered one of the most important anywhere, by both enthusiasts and experts alike.

Through Lotusland's collaborations with individual horticulturalists and other institutions worldwide, the garden often receives rare or exotic seeds or plants that are new to the collections. Some of the specimens are not chosen to be added to the garden immediately and are grown and nurtured by the garden's horticultural experts, sometimes for up to a decade or longer.

OPPOSITE: Madame Ganna Walska, shown here in 1957, surrounded by her beloved—and iconic—cactus and *Euphorbia* collections, created a series of idiosyncratic gardens at the estate from 1941 to 1984.

Lotusland opened its gates to the public in 1993, nine years after the death of the estate's owner Ganna Walska, referred to by all as "Madame." She was an adventurous, inquisitive, and charismatic spiritual seeker who lived a life of legend. Born Hanna Puacz in Brest-Litvosk, Poland, in 1887, she eloped with a Russian baron in 1907 at age twenty. After changing her name in 1914, Madame

Walska, as she was now known, moved to New York and in the ensuing years shuttled between New York and Paris, performing as an opera singer and marrying five more times after the baron's death.

Already a student of yoga, astrology, meditation, telepathy, numerology, Christian Science, and Rosicrucianism, around 1933 Madame Walska embarked on her search for the "great purpose" of her life, studying hypnotism and Indian philosophies. Her studies led her to meet Theos Bernard, a similarly charismatic individual and yogi who was one of the earliest, and most famous, proponents of Hatha yoga in the West.

Bernard became Walska's final husband in 1942. The previous year, Walska purchased the property then known as Cuesta Linda, which they intended to serve as a retreat for Tibetan lamas; together, they renamed it Tibetland. Alas, World War II scuttled their plans to bring the lamas to America, and in 1946 Walska and Bernard divorced. Madame promptly renamed the estate Lotusland after the sacred aquatic plant that flourished there.

Immediately after acquiring the land in 1941, Madame Walska hired the renowned landscape architect Lockwood de Forest, Jr. to renovate the orchards and create a number of individual garden spaces on the property. Following de Forest's deployment to World War II in 1943, Ralph Stevens, son of the property's

ABOVE: An illustration, c. 1959, by artist Joseph Knowles Sr., inspired the Aloe Garden's clamshell fountains (seen on page 96). **OPPOSITE**: Madame Walska kept an extensive collection of scrapbooks on topics that interested her. Out of more than 200, this assortment highlights her passion for garden information and inspiration. Lotusland's archives also store drawings by her longtime collaborators and other garden-related ephemera. The Bakelite necklace (top right) is a piece Madame owned that was created by the artist and designer Erté, now in the possession of her niece, Hania Puacz Tallmadge, who lived on the property during her young adult years.

WINDMILL PALM (Trachycarpus)
Here is a fine palm tree for use where a hint of the tropics is desired. Although slow growing, it is one of the toughest in this family. Growing to 25 or 30 feet, it is not too particular as to soil conditions and withstands drought.

Palms are excellent street trees as they are relatively clean and won't try to take over an area. This clump of Phoenix reclinata, above, accents a corner in San Marino

Two clumps of lady palms, Rophis humilis, provide design and color contrast against wall of house designed by Buff, Straub & Hensman. Palm attains a height of 18 ft. R. excelsa may be used where a shorter species is desired

The TRAVELERS PALM Madagascar
ITS 30-FOOT-HIGH FAN IS VISIBLE FOR MILES -- AND THE BASE OF EACH STALK HOLDS A QUART OF COOL WATER FOR THE PARCHED WAYFARER!

Cycas : l'arbre mangeur de jeunes filles

Viewed from underneath, some palms make a striking pattern against the sky. This is true especially of the Livistonas. At left you see an L. decipiens photographed in the botanical gardens at the Huntington Memorial Library in San Marino, the Southland's largest collection of palms

Impenetrable foliage of bamboo clump (top) and the traveler's tree, Ravenala madagascariensis which always faces east and west and will yield a pint of cool water if punctured

Tough, readily available sabal palms, right, are grouped picturesquely before house in the Spanish style. Species is notable for interesting pattern of its petioles, or bases of fronds, which sometimes cr...

CANARY ISLAND DATE PALM (Phoenix Canariensis) Small fruit is not edible

Average Washingtonia palms develop rigidly straight trunks, but these two grew curved, so were just right for planting to extend over a poo...

MILES -- 10 TIMES THE CIRCUMFERENCE OF THE EARTH! HE VOTED IN 76 CONSECUTIVE ELECTIONS

THE BUILDER'S PALM Madagascar
ITS LEAVES ARE USED FOR THATCHING THE ROOF AND AS DISHES, PLATES AND SPOONS. ITS LEAF STEMS MAKE THE FRAMEWORK OF WALLS AND PARTITIONS, ITS LUMBER PROVIDES THE WALLS -- ITS BARK IS USED FOR FLOORINGS. IT IS ALSO CALLED THE TRAVELER'S PALM, BECAUSE AT THE BASE OF EACH STALK IS A QUART OF COOL WATER

QUEEN OR COCOS PALM Native to Brazil

Abyssinian banana and two rubber trees form the corner planter tried at the rear of the yard, backed by joining walls of concrete blocks

Contemporary building backs dramatic grouping of bamboo palms, redwoo... ...ding accents pampas gr...

Lotus, especially the large-leaved Egyptian type, would be valuable if only for its interesting leaves—ruffled parasol bloom inside out. Raindrops scoot off the leaves as from duck's back. Plants are hardy if roots are protected from freezing, bloom all summer. Seed pods are huge shak...

Lotus lifts its fragrance to the air ...lection of its pink petals upon the water."

PAPYRUS PLANTS on the Lualaba River in the Congo FLOAT IN CLUSTERS SO LARGE THEY RESEMBLE ISLANDS

A GIANT LOTUS PLANT-- grown in Umicho village, Japan, HAD A LEAF THAT WOULD COVER A 9-FT.-SQUARE ROOM ...

The Oldest Flower
Buried 2,000 years, lotus seed finally gets chance to bloom

Most lotus plants bloom every year, but the lotus above waited 2,000 years to produce its first blossom. Until a year and a half ago its seed had lain in a neolithic canoe which was buried beneath 18 feet of earth in a peat log not far from Tokyo. While digging for the peat, some Japanese workmen discovered the canoe and turned it over to some archaeologists. The archaeologists in turn discovered the 2,000-year-old seed and turned it over to Dr. Ichiro Ohga, who placed it in a tank of water to see if it would sprout. This summer, after a year of germination and growth, the seed developed into a beautiful pink flower. Although it is the oldest seed ever to bloom, Dr. Ohga, who has had similar success with 1,000-year-old seeds, whelms... "It's quite a flower," he said, "but not different from lotuses today."

MADAME WALSKA

NT LOTUS WAS FULLY OPEN BY 9 A.M., CLOSED BY 5 P.M. THE FLOWER BLOOMED FOR FOUR DAYS, THEN ITS PETALS DROPPED

original owners and then the Santa Barbara Parks Superintendent came on board, and over the next decade he, alongside Madame Walska, developed many of Lotusland's iconic landscape features. Future collaborators included William Paylen, Frank Fujii, and stonemason Oswald Da Ros. Charles Glass and Robert Foster made important contributions in the 1970s and 1980s, both as designers and curators, though Madame always retained the title "head gardener."

Over the course of forty-plus years, the once-native land that had been home to a commercial nursery for its initial use, was transformed into a garden paradise full of staggering natural wonders. Unlike many of the world's well-known and respected botanic gardens, Lotusland was not created under the aegis of a governing body or led by specialists in the field of horticulture. And while Madame Walska was not professionally trained in the field of botany, she could certainly not be considered a hobbyist gardener. She led by instinct and with a passion for the best (and most!) collectable plants on the planet. She sought out, consulted, and engaged the best experts in their fields to help shape and realize her vision for Lotusland, but it was always her distinctive vision. Her maximalist ethos, typified by signature gestures such as the profuse grouping of single specimens, the assemblage of massive varieties of plant families, and the deployment of extravagant, dramatic gestures, is part of what makes Lotusland so unique among botanic gardens throughout the world. Eye-catching and unorthodox garden adornments, such as large chunks of colored glass, gems and minerals, and giant clam shells, appear in the landscape and contribute to the estate's visual excitement.

And yet, unlike a traditional museum with static installations, Lotusland's living collections are ever changing and ever evolving. Plants mature, plants die. Room has to be made for exciting and scientifically more important new additions. Since the late 1990s, the garden's living collections have grown significantly, and several gardens have been restored and reimagined to support their function in this now public garden. Today, the goal of its stewards is to preserve and enhance the historic estate and gardens of Madame Ganna Walska, and to develop conservation and sustainable horticulture programs that educate and inspire, while advancing global understanding and appreciation of plants and environmental responsibility.

OPPOSITE: Lotusland is sited on a gently sloping hill, and spans thirty-seven acres. With the area's coastal Mediterranean climate—and almost 300 days of sunshine a year— the property has been a testing ground for experimenting with new types of tropical and subtropical plants since 1882. Illustrated map by Janice Blair.

INSECTARY
GARDEN

THE
ORCHARDS

FERN
GARDEN

OLIVE ALLÉE

DUNLAP CACTUS
GARDEN

PARTERRE &
ROSE GARDEN

TOPIARY
GARDEN

UPPER BROMELIAD
GARDEN

THEATRE
GARDEN

LOWER BROMELIAD
GARDEN

WATER
GARDEN

SUCCULENT
GARDEN

ALOE
GARDEN

BLUE
GARDEN

CYPRESS
ALLÉE

SUCCULENT
GARDEN

WATER
STAIRS

JAPANESE
GARDEN

CYCAD
GARDEN

AUSTRALIAN
GARDEN

TROPICAL
GARDEN

LIFE AT LOTUSLAND

From the moment one arrives at Lotusland, it is clear that the experience will be like no other; this is not simply an historic estate transformed into a formal botanic garden.

Greeting one immediately at the entrance to Lotusland on Sycamore Canyon Road are two enormous, ancient Chilean wine palms (*Jubaea chilensis*) flanking either side of the gate. These epic specimens were planted by one of the property's earliest owners, nurseryman Ralph Kinton Stevens, in the late nineteenth century. Crossing through and proceeding up the drive to the eight-thousand-square-foot pink stucco structure that was once the main house and now serves as the administrative offices, visitors are already introduced to dizzying array of aloes, palms, bamboo, and especially cacti, providing just a glimpse of the wonders that await once inside the gardens.

This passage along the three hundred-yard main drive reveals the complex layers of the more than 130-year horticultural history of the place now called Lotusland, one in which previous owners of the estate played key roles. The impressive residence, built in the Mediterranean Revival style that also gives nearby Santa Barbara its architectural identity, was commissioned by the estate's second owners, E. Palmer and Marie Gavit, and completed in 1920. Prominent architect Reginald Johnson designed the house, as well as the Santa Barbara Biltmore hotel, the city's downtown post office, and numerous other distinctive buildings.

While Madame Walska's indelible forty-plus year imprint on Lotusland is responsible for its position today as one of the most important botanic gardens in the world, its horticultural legacy actually began as early as 1882 when Stevens purchased the ninety-eight-acre parcel (originally part of a government land grant) to create what would become a thriving and far-reaching nursery business.

At the time Montecito was, if not exactly the untamed West, definitely not the cultivated enclave it is known as today. The property was originally dubbed Tanglewood by Stevens's wife Caroline Lucy, owing to the gnarled chaparral and density of California coast live oaks that dotted and, in places, choked the acreage. Like others before and multitudes following him, the British-born Stevens had been

OPPOSITE: *Agave gypsophila* is known for its wavy leaf margins and unusual yellow-orange flowers. **PREVIOUS SPREAD**: The main drive features stepped plantings of *Sedum pachyphyllum*, fox tail agave (*Agave attenuata*), and *Aloe salm-dyckiana,* which features tall inflorescences with dark red flowers. **PAGE 18**: The estate's historic gate is flanked by two Chilean wine palms (*Jubaea chilensis*) that date to the late 1800s and were planted by previous owner and nurseryman Ralph Kinton Stevens.

drawn to the area for its remarkable microclimate: a perpetual summer in which almost any plant from anywhere in the world can be coaxed to grow.

Stevens built a sandstone and wood shingle home on the property and propagated all manner of plants on the land. Indeed, in 1893, his was the first California nursery to issue a catalogue devoted solely to tropical and subtropical plants, and many of the garden's signature plantings, which formed the locus for gardens later developed by Madame Walska, were planted by him. Stevens died unexpectedly in 1896 and for the next seventeen years, his widow struggled to maintain the sizeable property before selling it in 1913.

When the Gavit family moved into their new home in 1920, they christened it Cuesta Linda, Spanish for "pretty hill." While the house was being constructed, the Gavits hired horticulturalist and landscape designer Peter Riedel to renovate the gardens, a task he was assisted in by Stevens's son, also named Ralph. Following the home's completion, the Gavits retained landscape architect Paul Thiene to design the formal gardens in traditional Italianate style, which largely remain intact

ABOVE: The historic residence, with its iconic pink stucco facade, is now home to Lotusland's administrative offices. **OPPOSITE**: Old man of the Andes (*Oreocereus celsianus*) is a cactus known for its white hairs, which are believed to protect it from sunburn and cold temperatures. **PREVIOUS SPREAD**: A blooming *Catalpa speciosa* tree and row of Kentia palms (*Howea forsteriana*) line part of the main drive. **OVERLEAF**: Madame Walska's passion for mass plantings is evidenced by a grouping of *Parodia leninghausii* in the foreground against a backdrop of South American cacti, including *Oreocereus celsianus*, *Espostoa lanata*, and *Oreocereus hendrcksenianus*.

Cheerful golden barrels (*Echinocactus grusonii*) were some of Madame Walska's favorite cacti, and they are sometimes referred to, in jest, as mother-in-law cushions. Despite the profusion and abundant displays of them at Lotusland, they are endangered in the wild. In the 1950s, Madame worked extensively with Antonia Crowninshield (1915–2005), a certified botanical field collector from Arizona who sourced many of the plants and other cacti and succulents for her through expeditions to Mexico. PREVIOUS SPREAD: Mounds of golden barrels surround a large cardon (*Pachycereus pringlei*), native to Baja, Mexico, and the tallest cactus species known. It is closely related to the saguaro (*Carnegiea gigantea*) from Arizona. The tall, double-stemmed columnar specimen is an old man cactus (*Cephalocerues senilis*), native to Guanajuato and Hidalgo, Mexico. OVERLEAF: Underneath the canopy of towering dragon trees (*Dracaena draco*), is a large candelabrum-shaped *Isolatocereus dumortieri* and even more eye-catching clusters of golden barrels.

"Living on this planet is not a reality but merely a passing moment in time and space allotted us for growth." —Madame Ganna Walska

at Lotusland today. In the mid 1920s, the Gavits engaged Santa Barbara architect George Washington Smith to assume responsibility for significant new features on the property, which included a separate dwelling addition for their daughter, the now-iconic pink wall that surrounds the estate, a horse stable, garages, living quarters for property staff, and a swimming pool with bathhouse. Smith's work reflects the Spanish Moorish elements still found today in the gardens of Lotusland, a complement and contrast to Johnson's Italianate-inflected designs.

Following the death of the Gavits, the estate was sold to Sir Humphrey Clarke, a British diplomat, in 1939. While the Clarkes made architectural changes, they seemed to exhibit little interest in altering the landscape, and in 1941, Ganna Walska acquired the property. Already by the summer of 1942, Madame had charged Lockwood de Forest with locating unique, mature cacti and other succulents to replace the traditional landscaping surrounding the main residence's entry. The unorthodox choice was highly unusual but very much in keeping with Madame Walska's idiosyncratic approach to design. Today, this remains one of the property's most arresting features, particularly the dramatic, twisting arms of *Euphorbia ingens* flanking the entrance, leading right up to the front door. It is almost as if the living elements from outdoors are prepared to move in and occupy the house itself. This symbiotic metaphor is an apt description of the relationship between the creator of the gardens at Lotusland, the designers who followed, and the gardens themselves—each one reflecting and informing the other.

OPPOSITE: *Euphorbia resinifera* is a low-mounding plant native to the Atlas Mountains in Morocco. OVERLEAF: Lotusland is known for its unique juxtapositions of foliage and color. Large, blue-green *Agave americana (foreground)*, ghostly *Euphorbia ammak* 'Variegata' *(middle right)*, and Senegal date palms (*Phoenix reclinata*, top right)—with their feathery fronds and clusters of hanging fruit—stand out amidst a sea of green textures.

Euphorbia mammillaris 'Variegata' (above) and *Euphorbia clandestina* (opposite) are complemented by large uncut chunks of amethyst. Madame Walska used pieces of the semiprecious stone, as well as rose quartz and other minerals and crystals, throughout the property as unpredicted decorative elements. (Spiritual in nature, she also may have been drawn to their energy and healing properties.) **OVERLEAF**: Weeping *Euphorbia ingens* are some of Lotusland's most beloved plants. **PAGES 44-45**: The oldest dragon tree in the Dracaena Circle dates to the 1890s. **PAGES 46-47**: The great lawn.

THE PALMS

Although ubiquitous to southern California and a universal symbol of the tropics, where they do indeed thrive, palms of every genus can be found in habitats ranging from rainforests to deserts. Still, only one species—the California Fan Palm (*Washingtonia filifera*)—is native to the state. At Lotusland, a staggering variety of palms play significant roles in the overall landscape. The garden has approximately 170 species of palms in its collection, with two areas dedicated specifically to the plants: the Shade Palm Garden, which holds about forty species of the genus *Chamaedorea*, and the Palmetum, a concentration of more than sixty different types of palms, many of which can only be found in this part of the property.

In the true spirit of Madame Walska's more-is-more philosophy, palms are found everywhere at Lotusland, adding texture and character throughout, acting at times as the dominant focal point; and at other times, serving as the supporting players in a dramatic visual scenario. Certain palms also stand out for their maturity (more than fifty specimens on the property are more than one hundred years old) and their colossal stature, including the two iconic Chilean wine palms (*Jubaea chilensis*) that stand sentinel at Lotusland's front gate. These magnificent trees, like many at Lotusland, were planted in the late 1890s by the property's first owner, nurseryman Ralph Kinton Stevens. They are now protected in their native habitats, as they were endangered in their home country of Chile for many years (and are still vulnerable there), making those at Lotusland all the more important. These advanced specimens contribute to Lotusland's overall allure and appeal. Walking through the garden, one is immersed and humbled by the scale—and volume—of these wise, wild, and wonderful trees.

More than fifty mature and majestic palms on the property date to the late 1800s when Ralph Kinton Stevens operated his tropical nursery business on the property.
OPPOSITE: Senegal date palms (*Phoenix reclinata*) feature large, graceful fronds.
OVERLEAF: A rare *Jubaeopsis caffra*, native to South Africa, frames a view of the Japanese Garden in the distance. **PAGE 52**: A cluster of red fruit on a female *Chamaedorea microspadix*. **PAGE 53**: Senegal date palm.

Madame Walska's friend, Otto Martens, was a local palm expert who encouraged her interest in the plants and persuaded her to introduce many unusual species to the property in the 1960s. **TOP ROW, LEFT TO RIGHT**: Jelly palm (*Butia capitata*); *Brahea nitida*; *Brahea aculeata*. **BOTTOM ROW, LEFT TO RIGHT**: *Butia capitata*; *Jubaea chilensis* x *Butia capitata*; Bismark palm (*Bismarckia nobilis*).

WATER GARDEN

Throughout the year, in every season, something is always in bloom at Lotusland. For visitors who tour the gardens from mid-June through early September, the display of hundreds of strawberry-pink Asian lotus (*Nelumbo nucifera*) blossoms erupting in the Water Garden is truly a breathtaking sight to behold. Lotuses are the gems of the aquatic world, and the estate's namesake plant never fails to awe in its brilliant display, a reminder that Madame Walska was inspired to change the name of the property from Tibetland to Lotusland due to the profusion of the lotus flowers growing in what is now the Japanese Garden pond.

The Water Garden's centerpiece is the pond in which the aquatic specimens reside, which was the former swimming pool installed by the Gavit family in the 1920s. The rectangular lotus pond is flanked on either side by organically shaped water lily ponds filled with equally beautiful coral, salmon, white, and yellow lilies, including Nymphaea, Nuphar, and Victoria. This enchanting scene is complemented by a pink bath house designed by George Washington Smith in 1925, which serves as a charming backdrop.

Mysterious, exotic, and celebrated for their beauty, the lotus is among the oldest flowering plants in existence. As such, they possess a rich history of deep social and spiritual significance in both the ancient and modern worlds. In ancient Greece, the lotus flower represented innocence, purity, and modesty. In Hinduism and Buddhism, it is considered the most sacred flower, and is a symbol of life, renewal, and transcendence. Like most culturally meaningful plants and animals, this symbolism is rooted in actual elements of

OPPOSITE: The garden's namesake sacred lotus (*Nelumbo nucifera*) serves as a symbolic reminder of hope and renewal. **PREVIOUS SPREAD**: When Madame Walska purchased Lotusland, the pool was in poor shape, so she converted it to a water garden by filling it with soil and gravel to bring the water level to its current three-foot depth. On each side of the rectilinear pool are curvilinear ponds featuring water lilies. **PAGE 57**: Overlooking the pool, one sees the Cypress Allée path, on axis, in the distance—a vestige of the more formal garden design implemented by the Gavit family in the 1920s. **OVERLEAF**: The George Washington Smith-designed bath house provides a romantic backdrop against the blooming lotuses.

its biology. The lotus starts as a seed in the mud. It grows many rhizomes before emerging into the air and blooming, revealing a beautiful flower unmarred by the muddy waters from which it arose, and in which it is still rooted. The mud is said to symbolize the basis of life—the physical world—while the flower represents spiritual enlightenment. Its life cycle, growing out of murky waters into the air, symbolizes transcendence, another reason Madame Walska may have been drawn to the plants.

Lotus blossoms are beautiful and may appear delicate, but they are remarkably resistant and sturdy plants. They can live under the surface of frozen ice and can bloom in the blistering sun, when other flowers simply wilt. Scientific study has revealed that lotus seeds submerged in lake beds more than one thousand years can still germinate and bloom, a cycle of rebirth that no doubt contributes to its role as a sacred plant. Metaphorically speaking, each lotus is "reborn" every day it is in flower; every evening, its blossom closes only to reemerge and open again the next day.

ABOVE: Madame Walska, c. 1958, surrounded by large Victoria lilies (*Victoria amazonica*). **OPPOSITE**: *Nymphaea* 'Wanvisa'. **OVERLEAF**: Purple globe-shaped blooms from Lily of the Nile (*Agapanthus praecox* ssp. *orientalis*) and spiky foliage from a pair of New Zealand flax (*Phormium tenax*) add texture and color. **PAGE 68**: *Nembulo nucifera*. **PAGE 69**: Duck weed (*Lemna minor*) and dried lotus pods skim the pond's surface. **PAGES 70-71**: The water garden at its peak summer splendor.

CYPRESS ALLÉE &
WATER STAIRS

In the 1920s, elaborate, formal gardens, often with Italian or Spanish flair or other European influences, were standard features for the grand estates of Montecito and throughout Southern California. These structured gardens were often defined by long, linear pathways, elaborate water features, and clipped parterres that reinforced a sense of procession. A geometric—and at Lotusland, decidedly Italianate—sensibility informed the design, with perpendicular axes and symmetrical elements used to shape these elaborate garden rooms. These rigidly adhered to standards left little room for spontaneity.

The Gavit family installed many formal garden features during their nearly twenty years at the estate beginning in the year 1919, including the Cypress Allée and the Water Stairs. The Cypress Allée is a three-hundred-foot-long brick walkway lined on either side by stately Italian Cypress trees, which culminates at an ornamental carved limestone wishing well. Extending at a right angle from there lie the Water Stairs, a series of fourteen basins fed by water from the well that gently cascades down from one level to the next. Lined on either side by ivy, paving stones, and linear hedges, the Water Stairs lead into the Japanese Garden, which, during the Gavit era and before Madame Walska's transformation, was an irrigation reservoir-turned-pleasure pond, complete with sailboat.

Unlike other parts of the gardens that Madame Walska dramatically redesigned to her own liking, these two spaces still retain the key features of their original design and must have resonated with her European sensibility. In a sense, the simplicity and structure of these spaces may feel a bit incongruous amidst the visual eclecticism of other Lotusland gardens, but these quiet oases are, like a rest in a musical composition, spaces that offer a moment of visual quiet before moving onto the generally more lively gardens at Lotusland. It is this balance of profusion and restraint that is, in effect, part of what gives the garden its magic.

OPPOSITE: At the time of Madame Walska's death in 1984, the Cypress Allée, which dates to the 1920s, was in disrepair. In 2008, the Cypress Allée was replicated with new rows of *Cupressus sempervirens* 'Glauca' trees and *Abelia* 'Edward Goucher' shrubs, restoring the area to its former grandeur.

ABOVE: The Water Stairs' stream originates from an original decorative spout.
OPPOSITE: Fourteen basins comprise the aquatic feature. Creeping thyme (*Thymus serpyllum* 'Elfin') grows amidst the sandstone paths. The arborvitae hedges are *Thuja occidentalis* 'Rushmore'.

ALOE
GARDEN

I n garden design, a frequently used sleight of hand is the technique of hide and reveal. It's the sublime art of making a small space feel infinitely larger, a clever method often used in the design of traditional Japanese gardens and used here to dramatic effect. Somewhat unexpectedly, it is employed with gracious subtlety and true aplomb in the Aloe Garden, where unusual specimens create a transportive, one could say magical, fairy-tale-like atmosphere. A casual walk through this surprisingly dense, yet soothing landscape reveals an unusual selection of specimens, often planted en masse. As one traverses the garden's slender brick paths, winding through its gracious switchbacks, the visitor is enveloped in an otherworldly landscape of towering tree aloes and large grugru palm, Chilean wine, and ponytail palms. For dramatic effect, multiple *Aloe barberae*, featuring immense, bulbous trunks, and occasionally reaching 30 feet (or higher) into the sky, provide a canopy of thick, mottled stems.

The unexpected theatricality of 167 taxa of aloe plants is evident in its variety: minuscule to gigantic, even everyday *Aloe vera*, which is perhaps the

ABOVE: A walk along one of the Aloe Garden's wandering paths reveals the range in size of the plants, from small, low, clumping forms to tall, tree-size specimens.
OPPOSITE: A vibrant *Aloe salm-dyckiana*. Aloes grown in Africa are pollinated by birds with long beaks called sunbirds; in the United States, hummingbirds take on the role.
PAGE 76: An *Aloe marlothii* hybrid. **PREVIOUS SPREAD**: The garden during its winter blooming season. **OVERLEAF, LEFT TO RIGHT**: *Aloe confusa* and *Aloe lutescens*.

most commonly known species as both as a household plant and renowned for its medicinal qualities. Contrary to popular belief, only a fraction of aloes possess those curative attributes. Most come from Africa, Madagascar, and the Arabian Peninsula; South Africa in particular is home to more than half of the known varieties. Montecito's Mediterranean climate is an appropriate substitute to that of their origins, allowing most to thrive. Being immersed in the Aloe Garden is a transportive—and, in a way, fantastical experience—yet at certain moments, one other detail adds to the drama. Their main blooming season, from December to March, coincides with the region's fleeting rainy season, and the glistening water drops on the aloes' high-voltage red, yellow, and orange flowers amplifies the magic there, making their presence all the more effervescent—and amplifying their radiant blooms' ephemeral nature.

Midway through the journey into this captivating garden, one discovers the spectacular kidney-shaped abalone pool. Revealing itself as an epic surprise, like a mystical oasis in a desert fantasy, it is adorned with abalone shells fashioned into flowering blossoms that surround its perimeter. Triple-tiered fountains created from gigantic *Tridacna gigas* clam shells add visual dynamism and sonic solace. During the Aloe Garden's creation, as Madame Walska turned her attention to redesigning the previously existing pool, she presented her longtime gardener and collaborator Oswald de Ros with a white porcelain teacup filled with water, which was her inspiration for the pool's unusual, luminescent hue.

The spiritually enlightened Madame Walska also requested that all soil and stonework be moved by hand, and that no heavy machinery be used in its 1975 reconfiguration. This sensitivity to the earth, treating it as a living organism to be thoughtfully cultivated, is, at Lotusland, both palpable and ineffable. As such, this garden with its surprising transitions and reveals, where one travels down meditative, almost secret paths and then suddenly discovers an immense bright and lively pool, can be considered a liminal space, one that hovers between what is tangible and what is imagined, wholly real and completely other-worldly.

OPPOSITE, CLOCKWISE FROM TOP LEFT: French aloe (*Aloe pluridens*), Queen of the Night cactus (*Selenicereus hamatus*), and two perspectives of the branching inflorescences of *Aloe salm-dyckiana*. **PREVIOUS SPREAD**: Masses of *Aloe salm-dyckiana* surround the base of a giant *Jubaea chilensis*. **OVERLEAF**: Mount Elgon aloe (*Aloe elgonica*) is a clump-forming plant from Kenya that is blushed with pink as new leaves emerge.

In garden design, a frequently used sleight of hand is the technique of hide and reveal ... the sublime art of making a small space feel infinitely larger. Somewhat unexpectedly, it is employed with gracious subtlety and true aplomb in the Aloe Garden, where unusual specimens create a transportive ... magical, fairy-tale-like atmosphere.

"Now the word 'impossibility' does not exist in my vocabulary anymore. Nothing is impossible!" —Madame Ganna

JAPANESE GARDEN

Peace, tranquility, and harmony are hallmarks of the traditional Japanese garden, as is the seeming simplicity that belies the careful thought that goes into its planning and care. Covering more than 1.5 acres, the Japanese Garden at Lotusland is also the largest of its themed landscapes. An important, historical example of the type of Japanese-style garden built on American private estates throughout the late nineteenth and early twentieth centuries, Lotusland's Japanese Garden is one of the few Japanese-style gardens open to the public between Los Angeles and the Bay Area.

The garden's main focal point, the reflecting pond, was originally created by Ralph Kinton Stevens in the 1880s. Located on one of the lowest points of the property, it was used as a reservoir for Stevens's nursery business and was never originally designed to be an aesthetic focal point. Nonetheless, it was already densely filled with Asian lotuses when Madame Walska bought the

ABOVE: The garden's torii gate entrance welcomes visitors through a gateway symbolic of the passage from the secular to sacred world. OPPOSITE: A grove of Japanese cedars (*Cryptomeria japonica*), alongside the gurgling stream, are pruned in the *niwaki* style, a technique similar to bonsai. PREVIOUS SPREAD: The garden features more than thirty antique *ishi-doro*, or stone lanterns. OVERLEAF: The reflecting pond features koi, lotuses, water lilies, and Japanese irises. The island is graced by a Japanese black pine (*Pinus thunbergii*).

estate, and once she conceived of a Japanese-style garden around the pond, work ensued with stone mason Oswald de Ros and gardener Frank Fujii, the latter of whom continued to be associated with the project for the next forty years. (Fujii's father, Kinzuchi, was the mastermind behind the Storrier Stearns Japanese Garden, established in Pasadena, and contributed to the Japanese Garden at San Francisco's Golden Gate Park.)

Fujii balanced Madame Walska's flair for the dramatic with his penchant for simplicity, advocating a harmonious balance of plantings, stones, and other natural and man-made elements. Design principles and techniques reflect the Edo-era style strolling garden, including *shakkei*, where the illusion of space is manipulated to capture a distant view and make it an integral part of the immediate landscape. The sleight of hand works beautifully to create a microcosm of natural beauty. Cedars, pines, and other conifers reinforce an Eastern sensibility, while Moonrise Japanese maples and Akebono cherry trees and Chinese fringe trees add texture and color that evolves throughout the year.

An inveterate collector in all areas of her life, Madame Walska amassed a collection of more than thirty Japanese stone lanterns, or *ishi-doro*, which are placed artfully throughout the garden. Following a multi-year renovation to make the garden more welcoming and accessible, it reopened in 2019. While it still reflects Madame Walska and Fujii's original version, it now incorporates some of their initial plans that were never fully executed, including a *miwatasu*—a scenic overlook that offers expansive views of the reflective pond, which teems with koi—as well as an open-air pavilion and lotus viewing deck.

OPPOSITE: The sound of the waterfall adds a soothing sensory experience. PREVIOUS SPREAD: The *karesansui* is a dry landscape garden added during the 2019 renovation. OVERLEAF: Arched bridges are often a signature of Japanese gardens. The refurbished pond and fully accessible paths are some of the features added during the garden's 2017-2019 renovation, a collaboration between Lotusland staff, Arcadia Studio, and Comstock Landscape Architecture. PAGES 112-113: *Nymphaea* 'Clyde Ikins' water lilies have a soft peach tinge. 114-115: The Japanese pavilion is composed of Alaskan yellow cedar. 116-117: The structure is a traditional design and acts as a contemplative space, offering expansive views of the garden from its high hillside perch. PAGE 118: Madame Walska requested that a fresh bloom be placed in the Buddha's hands each day, a practice that continues today. PAGE 119: Spineless bramble fern (*Hypolepis tenuifolia*).

Peace, tranquility, and harmony are hallmarks of the traditional Japanese garden, as is the seeming simplicity that belies the careful thought that goes into its planning and care.

OPPOSITE: A thick forest of *Phyllostachys bambusoides*. PREVIOUS SPREAD: Japanese maples are known for their fine leaf texture. OVERLEAF, LEFT TO RIGHT: *Ajuga reptans* 'Black Scallop'. Pieces from two broken antique *ishi-doro* were recycled to create this unique lantern.

ABOVE: A great egret. **OPPOSITE**: A forest of black bamboo (*Phyllostachys nigra*) frames a view of the Japanese Garden and a majestic native coast live oak (*Quercus agrifolia*).

AUSTRALIAN GARDEN
AND PLANTS

Lotusland's gardens are known for their dramatic flair, but not every space displays unbridled exuberance at first glance. One of the most understated landscapes is the Australian Garden. However, upon closer inspection, individual plants and their minute features reveal a world of detail as awe-inspiring as the garden's more overt displays. Created in 1993, when the grounds first opened to the public, plantings exclusively native to the southern hemisphere were selected to soften and screen the public parking area and anchor the new visitor's center. Designed in collaboration with landscape architect Sydney Baumgartner, the area was developed within a mature eucalyptus grove, with some trees reaching as high as 130 feet tall. On a windy day, the susurrous sound of tall grass trees and the rustling of eucalyptus leaves brings a hushed calm to the bustling area. The garden gives a nod to Madame Walska's preferred method of planting with its grouping of large masses of plants, all of which hail from climate zones in Australia that are similar to that of Montecito. Feathery and sometimes delicate textures demand further examination: *Callistemon* 'Cane's Hybrid' with its pink bottlebrush-type blooms, *Grevillea* 'Moonlight' and its cylindrical inflorescences of ivory-color flowers, and Sea Urchin Hakea (*Hakea petiolaris*) with its globular clusters that resemble, yes, sea urchins. When blooming in June, a flamboyant flame tree (*Brachychiton acerifolius*) punctuates the otherwise quiet landscape with its fiery luminescence. Tea trees (*Leptospermum laevigatum*) native to the coastal dunes of southeastern Australia blanket a gracious arbor with textural, shaggy bark trunks and gnarled branches. The Australian Garden is a visitor's first encounter at Lotusland, and its quiet elegance may belie the wonder and awe that awaits. Its small details are worth seeking out; they are every bit as stunning as the garden's grander gestures and help create an ideal place for lingering longer.

OPPOSITE: *Xanthorrhoea preissii* is a slow-growing evergreen woody perennial that blooms only after it has matured (between seven to ten years of age).

TOP ROW, LEFT TO RIGHT: *Callistemon* 'Cane's Hybrid' features brush-like flowers and is often referred to as Cane's bottlebrush. Forest oak (*Allocasuarina torulosa*) features weeping fine-textured foliage. Lacebark tree (*Brachychiton discolor*). BOTTOM ROW, LEFT TO RIGHT: Sea urchin hakea (*Hakea petiolaris*) is native to the Darling Range, east of Perth. Leathery seed pods of Illawarra flame tree (*Brachychiton acerifolius*). Spidery flowers of *Grevillea* 'Moonlight'.

TROPICAL GARDEN

With its profusion of plants and foliage creating a jungle-like atmosphere, a stroll through the Tropical Garden can feel as much like an expedition through the depths of the Amazon rainforest as a leisurely stroll through a cultivated garden. The only indication that one isn't lost in nature or hasn't been transported to the Jurassic era is the tidy path that leads through it, and the fantastical hanging baskets of epiphyllums suspended overhead, their long, fleshy stems dangling toward the ground. In May and June, the shockingly vibrant blooms of these orchid cacti, as they are known, dot the garden. Although quite unlike the spiky, rigid cacti with which most of us are familiar and technically not orchids at all, these plants do, like orchids, grow on host plants and, like other bromeliads, take their nutrition from leaf mold and other organic waste.

Thriving under the dense tree canopy and among other exotic foliage, these tropical marvels compete for attention—and water and sun—with various palms, ferns, and other fascinating specimens such as the *Monstera deliciosa* that carpet the ground and clamber their way up the surrounding trees. The swiss cheese plant, as it is commonly known, is indeed a monster of a plant. Native to tropical rain forests throughout Mexico and Central America, its liana (a woody vine) can grow to lengths of up to sixty feet or more as it makes its way into the overhead trees, and has leaves that can grow to over three feet wide. The characteristic slits and holes found in the bold leaves are not just decorative, but practical, allowing rain and light to pass through to otherwise hidden parts of the plant.

OPPOSITE: The spathe and spadix of a Swiss cheese plant (*Monstera deliciosa*) are as unusual as its bright waxy leaves punctuated by natural leaf holes. **OVERLEAF**: A profusion of *Monstera deliciosa* and a cluster of lady palms (*Rhapis excelsa*, at right) contribute to the jungle-like atmosphere. **PAGE 136**: The leaf of an Abyssinian banana (*Ensete ventricosum*). **PAGE 137**: Epiphyllums, hanging from the trees in baskets, are cacti that feature show-stopping blooms in an array of colors, including red, white, yellow, pink, and orange.

CYCAD
GARDEN

Cycads, a class of ancient, cone-bearing plants, might at first appear unlikely candidates for the intense ardor they inspire in the plant lovers and collectors who obsess over them. They don't produce flowers, they are woody and often squat, and their spiky fronds can inflict wounds. Nonetheless, they are among the most coveted species in horticulture, inspiring obsessive collectors to scour the world for a single plant and tempting brazen thieves to steal them in daring heists. Modern-day cycads have evolved over the past twelve million years, yet their ancestors date to the dinosaur era; today, they are also the world's most threatened plant group and, in the last two decades, a number of species have become extinct in the wild. It is estimated that more than sixty percent of cycads are threatened—from being endangered in the wild by habitat destruction through deforestation and agricultural clearing, as well as illegal harvesting.

ABOVE: Lotusland's cycad collection is considered one of the world's finest. This section features plants from South Africa and Mexico. **OPPOSITE**: *Dioon edule* is known for its elegant blue-green coloration. **PREVIOUS PAGE**: *Encephalartos natalensis* is a large-growing South African species with leaves up to ten feet long. **OVERLEAF**: Lotusland's trio of beloved *Encephalartos woodii*—dubbed the Three Bachelors—overlook the koi pond. Resembling palms, this species is extinct in the wild. A single male specimen was discovered in 1895, but since a female has never been located, there can be no sexual reproduction of it. The entire plant was removed between 1903 and 1916, consisting of seven offsets and four stems, and sent to the Durban Botanic Gardens in South Africa. From there, propagations were shared with botanic gardens around the world. All *Encephalartos woodii* that exist today are clones of that original.

The glacial pace at which some of them grow combined with the rarity of some species are among the qualities that make them so highly prized. This rarity makes the 450-plus specimens at Lotusland, representing almost half of the species known to exist, all the more valuable from both biological and conservation perspectives.

The cycad's singular qualities, combined with their bold, sculptural shapes, no doubt attracted Madame Walska's eye for the exotic and unusual and led her to devote her attention—and considerable resources—to preserve and showcase the elusive plants, creating a 1.5-acre garden featuring them solely. It was the last garden she fully designed and developed on the property.

Although she had already established a collection of cycads, she soon set her sights on the most exquisite and rare specimens of these ancient plants, and she and garden designer Charles Glass set out to develop a site for them. Creating the Cycad Garden at Lotusland required incredible resources, even by Madame Walska's standards, so on April 1, 1971, she put up for auction at the Parke-Bernet Galleries in New York some of the most significant pieces from her renowned jewelry collection. Netting $916,185, an extraordinary sum at the time, Madame channeled the funds partly into developing this oasis (hence the moniker "the million-dollar garden," to which it is sometimes referred).

Lotusland's collection is thought to be one of the most complete in any American public garden, with more than 150 species of cycads dotting the landscape, including three *Encephalartos woodii*, which is now extinct in the wild. Lotusland cares for many species of threatened cycads, including five species in the collection that are believed to be extinct in the wild, underscoring the important work in conservation that is done here.

The Cycad Garden is not only visually arresting for its stark landscape, but also for the physical response it prompts—due to its lack of the overhead tree canopy that shelters most of Lotusland, the garden can suddenly feel up to twenty degrees warmer on a sunny day. Wandering into this primordial garden, with its profusion of assertive, sculptural shapes, is a sensory experience unlike any other at Lotusland.

OPPOSITE, CLOCKWISE FROM TOP LEFT: *Encephalartos natalensis. Encephalartos ferox* features unusual bright orange-red cones and glossy leaves with some of the sharpest lobes. *Encephalartos lanatus* is best known for its wooly cone as well as having adapted to survive its habitat's annual fire season in South Africa. *Lepidozamia peroffskyana* is native to eastern Australia and can grow to be massive, up to twenty-three feet tall. Cones on female plants are some of the largest of all cycads and can weigh up to sixty pounds.

The genus *Macrozamia* is endemic to Australia. There are about forty species of the palm-like cycads. PREVIOUS SPREAD: A path leads past the arched leaves of a low-growing South African *Encephalartos longifolius* (in the foreground, at left) into a mass of *Dioon*, a genus native to Mexico and Central America.

ABOVE: The Cycad Garden includes an eye-catching shaving brush tree (*Pseudobombax ellipticum*); the ephemeral flowers from this plant, native to Mexico, last only one day.
OPPOSITE: *Encephalartos latifrons* is a critically endangered cycad in the wild, but a species survival plan is being enacted for its protection. The slow-growing plant hails from the Eastern Cape of South Africa.

TOP ROW, LEFT TO RIGHT: The sago palm (*Cycas revoluta*), is the most readily available cycad, although it is often mistaken as a palm. The arid habitat of eastern Oaxaca is home to *Dioon oaxacensis. Encephalartos arenarius* features spiky blue leaves and is native to the coastal sands of the Eastern Cape of South Africa; it's sometimes referred to as the dune or Alexandria cycad. BOTTOM ROW, LEFT TO RIGHT: The young leaves of *Ceratozamia latifolia* feature an unusual bronze color before turning dark green. *Encephalartos heenanii* is believed to be extinct in the wild of its natural habitat of South Africa and Eswatini. *Dioon rzedowskii* features large cones that last multiple years on the plant. It is endangered in its native habitat of Oaxaca. OVERLEAF, LEFT TO RIGHT: *Ceratozamia fuscoviridis* is an understory cycad that is critically endangered in the wild; new growth features bronze and brown coloration. *Encephalartos friderici-guilielmi* is unusual for the large number of cones it produces that persistently remain on the plant for years; male plants feature a yellow coloration along the leaves' margins as they mature.

152

SUCCULENT
GARDEN

The stunning diversity of gardens at Lotusland, from lush tropical environments to arid, desert-like settings, is a testament to the skillful planning that went into realizing them, and the amazing adaptability and resilience of so many of its species, particularly the succulents. The word "succulent" describes a wide variety of plants from spiky cacti and aloes to the popular little hens and chicks. And while most cacti are succulents, not all succulents are cacti. Succulents can be found everywhere throughout Lotusland, but there is one garden devoted exclusively to succulents other than cacti, euphorbias, and aloes: the Succulent Garden that is home to more than 170 species. This amazing group of plants has adapted to survive long periods of drought by storing large amounts of water in either their fleshy leaves, swollen stems, or enlarged roots, and because of this trait, they make ideal targets for attack by wildlife in dry environments. As a result, many succulents have developed ingenious defense mechanisms including spines, poisonous sap, and coloration that not only provide camouflage, but make

ABOVE: In addition to being an artful display, raised garden beds aid with soil drainage for the succulents, as overwatering can be damaging to them. **OPPOSITE**: Hybrids of *Echeveria agavoides*. **PREVIOUS SPREAD**: The succulent garden is home to more than 170 different species. **PAGE 157**: *Aeonium arboreum* 'Zwartkop' is heralded for its large rosettes and dramatic dark purple foliage that can appear almost black. **OVERLEAF**: *Echeveria elegans* is known for its silvery-green leaves.

The sheer range of these fascinating plants—whether they are small and compact or tall and spindly—lends them an appeal both curious and exotic.

them so distinctive. The sheer range of these fascinating plants—whether they are small and compact or tall and spindly—lends them an appeal both curious and exotic. Like many of the Lotusland gardens, this one dates to the 1940s, but in 1973 Charles Glass, the editor of *Cactus and Succulent Journal*, and Robert Foster, co-owner of Abbey Garden Cactus and Succulent Nursery and Abbey Garden Press, played a crucial role in its renovation and preservation when the two were successfully wooed, after multiple attempts by Madame Walska, to come work for her. Glass worked at the garden for a decade and spearheaded many important projects around the estate, including the creation of several gardens.

Today, a stroll through the Succulent Garden yields a surfeit of delights. Large stones and boulders set among lava rock and pitted San Felipe stone beds contain the plants and add texture and definition. The sandy path that meanders through it is lined with hundreds of sparkling large chunks of bluish-green slag glass, a byproduct of the bottles manufactured by California's Arrowhead Water bottling company. Other surprising elements coexisting with the succulents are the statuettes that populate the garden. Depicting mythological figures including Pan and Bacchus, they add a theatrical element, at once whimsical and classical.

OPPOSITE: Madagascar ocotillo (*Alluaudia procera*) features rounded leaves and sharp gray spines. In its native habitat, it can reach sixty feet tall.
OVERLEAF, LEFT TO RIGHT: Glistening aqua-colored slag glass lines the garden path. Aeoniums are fleshy succulents with leaves arranged in rosettes.

"It is through the stories we weave in our minds that all great things happen in the world. In order to create, we have to work out the story in our imagination."

—Madame Ganna Walska

BLUE GARDEN

It has been said that Madame Ganna Walska was an artist who used plants as her brush and the land as her canvas. Perhaps nowhere in Lotusland is that artistic sensibility—one could call it a painterly approach—as sensitively deployed as in the Blue Garden. Defined by a palette of powdery, silvery shades that encompass a staggering array of tonalities, this inviting garden features a surprising range of grasses, cedars, and palms that somehow unite to form a harmonious whole. The thought of a "monochrome" garden might at first seem a bit dull, for what do we think about when we think about gardens, if not a vibrant array of colors? But what makes the Blue Garden—

and the vogue for single color gardens that goes back to at least the nineteenth century—so compelling, is the richness, variety, and visual excitement that can be teased out of this singular approach.

The influential British horticulturalist and garden designer Gertrude Jekyll (1843-1932) was a keen advocate for single color gardens and by 1942, when Lotusland's original Blue Garden was begun under the direction of Lockwood de Forest, color-themed gardens were fashionable. The original garden was planted with traditional blue flowering plants: delphiniums, blue lilies, and blue hyacinths, amongst others. At the same time, de Forest designed and planted a "silver garden," which, with the addition of blue Atlas cedars by Madame Walska and Ralph Stevens in 1948, evolved into the Blue Garden. By the mid-1950s, Lotusland's Blue Garden was widely celebrated as one of the most fascinating gardens in California, populated by blue grasses, the Atlas cedars, blue Brahea fan palms, and a dazzling assortment of agave. In the present day, on a moonlit evening, the garden practically glows as light reflects off the icy-hued foliage. The interplay of texture and scale—from the tiny clumping fescue grasses to the monumental *Agave franzosinii* with its enormous, undulating leaves—is truly remarkable and a testament to the richness and variety that can be borne from restraint.

ABOVE: Madame Walska surrounded by silvery-blue agaves. **OPPOSITE**: *Agave franzosinii* and blue Atlas cedars (*Cedrus atlantica* 'Glauca') contribute to the Blue Garden's muted palette. **OVERLEAF**: A pair of *Agave franzosinii* frame a view of the great lawn and the Santa Ynez mountains in the distance.

ABOVE: The celestial globe came from Madame Walska's French château, Galluis, and was brought to Lotusland in the 1960s. It is paired with a similar terrestrial globe (seen on previous spread). OPPOSITE: Under a tall canopy of Chilean wine palms (*Jubaea chilensis*) and a majestic coast live oak (*Quercus agrifolia*), blue fox tail agave (*Agave attenuata* 'Boutin Blue'), Mexican blue palm (*Brahea armata*), and blue fescue (*Festuca ovina* var. *glauca*) contribute to the garden's magical coloration. OVERLEAF: *Agave franzosinii.*

BROMELIAD
GARDEN

Lush and dense, the Bromeliad Gardens at Lotusland are home to more than 320 of the innumerable cultivars, hybrids, and species known to exist. Incredibly adaptable and diversified plants—they can be found in dry deserts and wet rainforests, from the Andean Highlands of South America to the American South—bromeliads grow on the ground, hang in the air, and attach themselves almost anywhere and to anything upon which they can gain purchase. Perhaps the varieties most familiar to us, both of which are grown here, are the variegated verwion of the pineapple (*Ananas comosus*) and Spanish moss (*Tillandsia usneoides*). The former, which grows in the ground supported by thick fleshy leaves, is the rare bromeliad which produces edible fruit—one of the most common tropical fruits in the world.

The latter example bears the traits of the majority of bromeliads: it is an epiphyte, or plant that grows on another plant, but is not parasitic. Like the orchid, which is not a bromeliad, it gathers its nutrients from the air, rain, and debris that surround it.

The first Bromeliad Garden at Lotusland was created in 1967, with the assistance of Fritz Kubisch, an orchid specialist who owned Jungle Plants and Flowers in Culver City. At one point, Madame Walska financed Kubisch's expeditions to Mexico and Central America to collect bromeliads, many of which ended up in a garden underneath a large live oak tree next to the Pavilion. The tree canopy provided the perfect dappled light needed for their success. (Left in full sun, their leaves become scorched or bleached.) Once the plants became too overcrowded for the space, a second home was created for them, referred to as the Lower Bromeliad Garden. Among the many striking elements of the now mature spaces are the giant ponytail palms (*Beaucarnea recurvata*) that border the garden; the Spanish moss dripping from the limbs of oak trees; and the almost dizzying array of spiky, spindly, spiny, and showy plants that despite their variety, all belong to this same family of plant. While some of them are delicate and lacy, others, such as the tank bromeliads, are substantial and strong. Indeed, these plants form their own microcosms in the garden: their tightly packed leaves, spiraling out from the base, form reservoirs that trap water—up to two gallons each in the largest—which become home to all type of aquatic life, including fungi, algae, and protozoa, which in turn attract and support insects, spiders, and amphibious creatures including frogs and salamanders.

OPPOSITE: The radiating colors of *Neoregelia carolinae*. **PREVIOUS SPREAD**: Ponytail palms (*Beaucarnea recurvata*) feature a large, rounded caudex for storing water. Black-and-white photography (pages 180-181) highlights the cracks in their trunks, a characteristic of mature specimens, and a reason they're often referred to as elephant foot trees. **OVERLEAF**: The Lower Bromeliad Garden showcases the diversity and complexity of the plants, all of which are New World except for one species from west Africa. The dramatic display has been the life's work of Mike Furner, a Lotusland gardener for more than four decades.

"Time and circumstances permitting, I hopefully dreamt that if given all the opportunities I might fulfill my work to develop Lotusland to its maximum capacity into the most outstanding center of horticultural significance and of educational use."

—Madame Ganna Walska

Among the many striking elements ... are the giant ponytail palms (*Beaucarnea recurvata*) that border the garden; the Spanish moss dripping from the limbs of oak trees; and the almost dizzying array of spiky, spindly, spiny, and showy plants that despite their variety, all belong to this same family of plant.

OPPOSITE: Spanish moss (*Tillandsia usneoides*) is repurposed as a mane of hair on a garden ornament, offering a whimsical note. OVERLEAF: Two coast live oaks (*Quercus agrifolia*) provide the bromeliads with the filtered sunlight they require to avoid the burning or bleaching of their foliage.

THEATRE GARDEN

Theater and the landscape have been entwined since ancient times. One of the earliest known open-air theaters is found at the Acropolis in Greece, dating to around 525 BC, and in subsequent centuries, such theaters became a common feature, primarily in societies throughout the West. In seventeenth-century Italy, green theaters of the type found at Lotusland became customary for villas and estates. These sometimes-elaborate settings combining architectural and sculptural elements were often designed as much for their decorative qualities as their practical purposes. Of course, Madame Walska had a love of the stage, and at one time, she owned the Théâtre des Champs-Élysées in Paris. In 1929, she purchased her home in France, the Château de Galluis, and would sometimes perform from her balcony that, in the springtime, overlooked thousands of red and white tulips planted in honor of the colors of the Polish flag.

At Lotusland, the Theatre Garden is where Madame's love of the stage and gardening intersect; it bridges her dazzling past life in the public eye with her quiet second chapter devoted to creating and cultivating Lotusland's glorious gardens. Designed by Ralph Stevens, the three-tiered garden was created for its functional and aesthetic properties. With seating to accommodate one hundred guests, the Theatre Garden was the site of many musical performances during Madame Walska's time, a tradition that continues to this day. The sandstone blocks used to define the three tiers and form its seating came from nearby quarries. The plantings that delimit and shape the garden's structure include African fern pine (*Afrocarpus gracilior*), Variegated Japanese Sedge (*Carex morrowii* 'Aurea-variegata'), and African boxwood (*Myrsine africana*). Of course, the most prominent—and amusing—element in the garden is the eclectic assortment of miniature grotesques that populate it. These limestone characters, or "Venetian figures," as Madame Walska called them, are carved in the style of the commedia dell'arte. Several of these figures were rescued from her château in France when she fled during World War II, and others were acquired once she had settled at Lotusland.

OPPOSITE: In the Theatre Garden, clipped African fern pine (*Afrocarpus gracilior*) is treated as the wings of the "stage," while variegated Japanese sedge (*Carex morrowii* 'Aurea variegata') serves as the "stage lights." **OVERLEAF**: Stepped terraces designed by Ralph Stevens provide guests with seating while watching performances. The garden, built in 1948 and restored and redesigned in 1988 by Isabelle Greene, was one of the first to be constructed after Madame Walska bought the property.

ABOVE: At the onset of World War II, Madame Walska fled her estate in France to live in the United States. After the war, she was able to retrieve many of her belongings, including several stone figures, called grotesques, or, as she referred to them, "Venetian figures." A few date to the 1600s. OPPOSITE: The figures' exaggerated countenances and physical features lend an air of eccentricity and curiosity to the garden.

DUNLAP
CACTUS
GARDEN

Much of the joy, wonder, and surprise that comes from strolling through Lotusland arises when happening upon the many awe-inspiring transitions as one moves from garden to garden. Rarely does one environment flow simply and gently into the next. Instead, astonishing changes in scenery leave visitors spellbound by radical juxtapositions. One of the most thrilling, and finest, examples of such a shift occurs when visitors encounter the Dunlap Cactus Garden, which somehow magically combines the desert-like landscape of the American West with the feeling of an almost lunar landscape. Approaching it from the fairy-tale-like Topiary Garden, with its fanciful, clipped forms, or from the bucolic Olive Allée, with its feeling of the European countryside, entering this seemingly extraterrestrial world, punctuated by massive columnar cacti, is certainly a major shift in tone.

Lotusland's Dunlap Cactus Garden came into being in 2003, almost two decades after Madame Walska's passing, but one could say that it was her final opus. After all, conversations and negotiations between Madame and an inveterate collector of cacti began in 1966 when a mysterious letter arrived at the Sycamore Canyon Road estate stating a gentleman's wish to bequeath his astounding collection of cacti in San Diego County to Lotusland. At that time, Merritt "Sigs" Dunlap had already been developing this collection—first at his home in Glendale, then at another residence in Fallbrook—for thirty-seven years.

In a garden brimming with superlatives, what's so remarkable is that Dunlap's history with the cacti spanned seventy years: he acquired his first plant in 1929 and the last in 1999. Even more astounding is the fact that almost forty percent of his collection was grown from seed, a process he was passionate about. With plants like these, provenance is most important, and Dunlap procured seed or sourced small plants from only the most reputable nurseries, researchers, and explorers of the time. Irreplaceable cacti from the Galápagos came through the hands of David Walkington of Fullerton Arboretum and Yale Dawson, then director of Darwin Research Station; South American cacti from Hildegart Winter, sister of indefatigable explorer Friedrich Ritter; and additional rarities through famed botanist and nurseryman Harry Johnson, to name a few.

Fast forward to 1999 when Dunlap changed his bequest to a donation, hoping to see it fully installed at Lotusland in his lifetime. (He did, in 2003 at age ninety-seven—and celebrated his birthday there.) Paul Mills, now the Curator of Living Collections, and longtime Lotusland

OPPOSITE: *Armatocereus mataranus*, native to Peru, features segmented gray-green stems and can grow up to forty feet tall. **PREVIOUS SPREAD**: *Opuntia galapageia* is endemic to the Galápagos Islands; the cactus has evolved into a tree-like shape to avoid over-predation from giant tortoises and iguanas, which rely on cacti as a primary source of food on the islands. **OVERLEAF**: The slender, arching stems of octopus cactus (*Stenocereus alamosensis*) can reach thirty feet in length.

Plants in the Dunlap Cactus Garden are divided by
country of origin. This path leads through specimens from
Peru. OVERLEAF, LEFT TO RIGHT: The columnar *Echinopsis
tulhuayacensis* (center) is native to the Peruvian Andes.
The pad of an *Opuntia galapageia* var. *profusa* is laden with
emerging flowers. PAGES 214-215: Sun-soaking black slate
chips serve as mulch throughout the garden; in this area, it's
surrounding cacti that are primarily Argentinian in origin.

Astonishing changes in scenery leave visitors spellbound by radical juxtapositions. One of the most thrilling examples occurs when visitors encounter the Dunlap Cactus Garden...

Superintendent Esau Ramirez led the charge to get the collection moved to Lotusland by 2001. Preeminent landscape designer Eric Nagelmann spearheaded the garden's inimitable design and layout. Safely untangling the fragile plants and reimagining and repositioning them in their new home located 190 miles north of Fallbrook was no small feat. Weekly trips for much of 2001 ensued, and 530 plants across three hundred taxa were transported up the 101 freeway without mishap. Meticulous records were kept to document each and every cactus's exact orientation to the sun for replanting; when cacti are relocated, they must be replanted in their original orientation, as the southern-facing side of cacti becomes toughened in the sun, leaving their north sides susceptible to sunburn.

Since being replanted in Lotusland's one-acre site (in contrast to Dunlap's more compact garden), the collection has thrived, and then some—many have grown as much as ten to twenty feet! The Lotusland garden is designed around a geographical theme, just as it was at Dunlap's residence; most all cactus species originate in the Americas, with the exception of one species from western Africa, so a stroll through this remarkable garden allows one to essentially experience the plants growing in all the great deserts of the New World. But walking through this sea of hundreds of sinuous, spiky, stalky, soaring (and often intimidatingly thorny) varieties can have an overwhelming effect; learning that each and every plant has a very personal backstory, spellbinding. Case in point: Look for *Echinopsis spachiana*, more commonly known as the Golden Torch. It was Dunlap's very first cactus, procured in 1929. No doubt even Madame would be awestruck.

OPPOSITE: Cactus taxonomy and nomenclature are ever-evolving fields. *Borzicactus*, for instance, has now been lumped into the genus *Cleistocactus*. **PREVIOUS SPREAD**: Sun-soaking black slate chips serve as mulch throughout the garden; in this area, it's surrounding cacti that are primarily Argentinian in origin.

ABOVE: *Pilosocereus* feature abundant woolly hair and typically flower later in the day. OPPOSITE: Steps made from Arizona flagstone lead to a viewing platform. OVERLEAF: Dragon fruit (*Hylocereus undatus*), a vine-like cactus (at left), has climbed the trunk of a coast live oak (*Quercus agrifolia*) for support. *Furcraea bedinghausii* (at right) is often mistaken as an agave with its blue-green leaves, but is actually a large succulent native to southern Mexico. PAGES 222-223: A collection of *Echinopsis* hybrids with plants of *Cleistocactus* towering above.

ABOVE: *Echinopsis macrogona*, native to Bolivia, is difficult to find in the wild.
OPPOSITE: This *Echinopsis spachiana* was the very first cactus grown by Merritt Dunlap, dating to 1929. **OVERLEAF, LEFT TO RIGHT**: Red Torch cactus (*Echinopsis huascha*). *Cleistocactus samaipatanus*. *Cleistocactus* is a genus native to the mountainous areas of Argentina, Bolivia, Peru, and Uruguay. **PAGES 228-229**: A dynamic collection of *Cereus* cacti from South America.

OLIVE ALLÉE

One of Lotusland's simultaneously most grand and most unassuming processional spaces is the Olive Allée, where many different varieties of this ancient and deeply symbolic tree line a pathway on axis to the Parterre. At the end of the allée, and at the entrance to the Dunlap Cactus Garden, lies another of Lotusland's distinctive water features, a *bas-relief* sculpture carved in marble and mounted on a free-standing pink wall, which depicts a mythological hippocampus—half horse, half sea monster—from which water gushes into a shallow basin below. Large pomegranate shrubs and agaves flank either side of the wall. Like every garden at Lotusland, a stroll through this arresting landscape is a wholly sensory experience. The sound of water, the sharp fragrance in the air, and the crackle and crunch of dried leaves underfoot make it feel as if one is being transported to southern Italy or the Andalusian countryside. This is truly one of the places at Lotusland where the landscape seems most sympathetic to the architecture of the estate's residence.

The olive tree, with its Mediterranean origins, has almost unparalleled historic, cultural, and culinary significance. Originating at least twenty million years ago and first domesticated in Ancient Greece, olives and olive oil are recorded in literature's earliest documents. Olive oil, in addition to being a mainstay in many ancient cuisines, has also long been believed to be sacred and holy. The olive branch is recognized universally as a symbol of peace, and the fruit of these trees is a mainstay of diets throughout the world. Capping this list of remarkable attributes is the fact that olive trees are among the longest living trees known to us, with some specimens being estimated to live up to two thousand years. While the exact date and origin of the olive trees at Lotusland is not known, most of these majestic late nineteenth-century specimens were originally planted by Ralph Kinton Stevens as stock for his nursery business, and remain to this day.

OPPOSITE: The patinaed hippocampus fountain is the focal point at the end of the Allée.
OVERLEAF: The olive trees date back to the time Ralph Kinton Stevens was growing them for rootstock for his nursery business in the late nineteenth century. Research conducted by the University of Arizona in 2007 revealed that ten of the olive trees are 'Frantoio', a type grown for its fruity oil; two match the genotype 'Nevadillo', favored for its delicately flavored oil; and two 'Redding Picholine', which are commonly used as rootstock for other varieties. Several of the trees show an affinity for some European cultivars such as 'Black Italian' or another variety originating in Greece or Tunisia.

TOPIARY
GARDEN

Simply put, topiary is the not so simple art of pruning evergreen shrubs and trees into ornamental shapes, either geometric or playful. A practice dating back to ancient Rome, the popularity of topiary has ebbed and flowed over the centuries and enjoyed a resurgence in favor around the turn of the twentieth century, coinciding with the golden era of estate building in the United States. The Topiary Garden at Lotusland was created by Ralph Stevens and Madame Walska between 1955 and 1957 and was redesigned by landscape designer Lori Ann David in 2001. She replicated many of the original shapes found in the garden and added new ones, among them fanciful figures that delight visitors, such as a mythological hippocampus (half horse, half sea monster), a giraffe, a dancing bear, and a seal balancing a ball on its nose. Other recurrent forms include spiraling shrubs and geometric globes and cones.

The spectacular centerpiece of this already fantastical garden is an enormous, operational horticultural clock. Measuring twenty-five feet in diameter, at the time it was created in 1955 it was the largest such clock in America. Like many of these clocks, it originally had roman numerals for the hours, which Madame Walska had replaced with large signs of the zodiac, handmade of copper. Zodiac signs were designed and crafted by Madame Walska's right-hand-man Gunnar Thielst. The clock was renovated in 1998, restoring its plantings and grading to the original of succulents supported by crushed stone in varying bands of color. The Topiary Garden is linked to and on axis with the original Parterre, and while its high hedge border and low clipped shrubs preserve the more structured feel of the former space, its fanciful animal figures and other sculptural elements add a sense of fun and wonder. That ability to bring opposing elements into a harmonious whole, balancing the yin and yang, is a hallmark of so many gardens at Lotusland, and a reflection of its creator's spirit.

OPPOSITE: Forms include animals, such as a giraffe, and chess pieces, among others. PREVIOUS SPREAD: Whimsical shapes take on lifelike personalities, depending on the day's light and shadows. OVERLEAF: Topiaries have to be pruned in a way that insures the plant's health while they undergo continual and severe trimming. Eugenia (*Syzygium paniculatum*) and juniper (*Juniperus chinensis* 'Spartan') topiaries are set against a stepped hedge of *Pittosporum undulatum*. PAGES 240-241: The zodiac clock is twenty-five feet in diameter, and features low-growing succulents and copper zodiac signs that were crafted to replicate earlier schemes. It's bordered by a ring of blue chalk sticks (*Senecio mandraliscae*). PAGES 242-243: An aerial view of the Topiary Garden.

PARTERRE & ROSE GARDEN

Parterre, from the French meaning on the ground, commonly refers to a formal, ornamental garden on one level, arranged with multiple axes and extended crisscrossing paths that lead the eye to viewing points in the distance.

Designed by Paul Thiene for the Gavit family in the 1920s, Lotusland's Parterre and Rose Garden are defined by linear brick paths and symmetrical planting beds that give them a geometry and sense of formality largely absent from many of Lotusland's other gardens. Spanish and Italian inspirations and elements of Moorish and Islamic iconography inform the hardscape, including the eight-ray star fountain at the heart of the Parterre.

Many of the gardens at Lotusland are well known for the diversity and abundance of their exotic foliage. The Parterre and Rose Garden differ, however, by showcasing an explosion of singular flowering specimens, as with the massive display of floribunda roses that bloom for nearly ten months a year.

Low clipped shrubs flank the brick-paved walkways, while ten-feet-tall eugenia and pittosporum hedges provide an architectonic structure to the garden.

Beyond its formal aesthetic beauty, the Rose Garden is a prime example of Lotusland's dedication to sustainable gardening practices. Roses are known to be finicky even in the best circumstances, often succumbing to myriad diseases that are normally treated with chemical pesticides and fungicides. Here, however, everything is organic, including the compost tea regularly sprayed on the foliage to provide a film of beneficial living organisms that not only suppresses disease, but provides a steady source of nutrients. The tea does not kill pests or disease pathogens but is a highly effective protective measure. At the same time, organic additions to the soil, including alfalfa and fish and kelp mixtures, are added regularly, providing the roses with the nutrients they need to stay healthy and create their signature blooms and heady fragrances.

ABOVE: Madame Ganna Walska, c. 1958, along the Parterre. **OPPOSITE**: Water from an eight-point, star-shaped fountain (featuring Islamic iconography) flows into a shallow (Moorish) rill where it is transported and then deposited into another basin downstream. Towering birds of paradise (*Strelitzia nicolai*) add a layer of interest and texture behind the stucco wall.

ABOVE: A baptismal font filled with *Graptopetalum paraguayense* hybrid features pale trailing rosettes against a lush hedge of eugenia (*Syzygium paniculatum*).
OPPOSITE: The garden's fountain is graced by two sago palms (*Cycas revoluta*) and a pair of two mermen flanking a sculpture of Neptune, god of the seas. The ceramic bowl is Austrian. PREVIOUS SPREAD: The rose garden includes Julia Child, Hot Cocoa, and Livin' Easy varieties, all selected by master rosarian Dan Bifano and planted during a restoration of the garden in 2007.

THE ORCHARDS

Lotusland has two historic orchards that are home to more than a hundred deciduous and citrus trees. The orchards were already in place when Madame Walska acquired the estate, and she continued to expand and add to them, introducing more and more varieties of trees, particularly exotic fruits such as papaya and cherimoya, which are closely related to the more commonly familiar sweetsop and soursop. The deciduous orchard contains an astounding variety of trees including stone fruits such as peaches and plums, and pome fruits, including apples and pears, as well as a number of hybrids such as pluots, apriums, nectaplums, and plumcots. It also boasts persimmons, figs, pomegranate, avocado, and chestnut. The citrus orchard contains orange, lemon, lime, kumquat, grapefruit, and guava trees.

At the center of the citrus orchard—and perhaps its defining element—is the lemon arbor. Originally created in the 1920s, it was redone in 1988 with new Eureka lemon trees planted at each upright post. Over time, the trees have been cultivated to cover the arbor, creating a most arresting and dramatic promenade for the visitor. The types of orchards at Lotusland, which include a profusion of varieties of trees as opposed to "production" orchards, which feature a single or few varieties, were at one time referred to as "gentleman's orchards," and in the early teens and 1920s, were considered an amenity *de rigueur* for any great estate. Today, conservation and preservation are hallmarks of Lotusland's ethos, and the orchards offer several great examples of sustainable practices. Staff and volunteers take advantage of the delicious harvests from these trees and their fruits have been donated to members of the community through food banks and other charitable organizations. In addition, all areas of the orchards are heavily mulched, creating an active biological system that provides nutrient cycling, eliminating the need for fertilizing.

ABOVE: Madame Walska picks fruit from the lemon arbor, c. 1958. **OPPOSITE**: The arbor, covered by Eureka lemons (*Citrus limon* 'Eureka'), was originally built in the 1920s and replicated in 1988. It serves as the transition through the deciduous and citrus orchards from the Parterre to the Insectary Garden. **OVERLEAF**: Both the leaves and the flowers of trailing nasturtiums (*Tropaeolum majus*) are edible.

ABOVE: Underneath its leathery rind, Buddha's hand citrus (*Citrus medica* var. *sarcodactylis*) is all pith and does not have a juicy pulp. **OPPOSITE**: Mandarin orange tree (*Citrus reticulata*). **OVERLEAF, CLOCKWISE FROM TOP LEFT**: Fragrant white lemon blossoms attract pollinators in late winter. Arctic Star nectarines (*Prunus persica* var. *nucipersica*) are a low chill variety, ideal for Montecito's mild winter. Dancy mandarins (*Citrus reticulata* 'Dancy') are self-pollinating. Minnie Royal cherry trees (*Prunus avium* 'Minnie Royal') are often the last fruit to bloom and the first to ripen. Variegated lemon (*Citrus limon* 'Pink Lemonade'). Red Baron peach trees (*Prunus persica* 'Red Baron') are known for their showy red double blossoms. Yuzu citrus (*Citrus junos*) is highly aromatic. Tiger stripe variegated figs (*Ficus carica* 'Panache') feature yellow and green stripes on their skin and a magenta- or crimson-colored seeded pulp.

INSECTARY GARDEN

The Insectary Garden may look like nothing less than a beautiful flower garden, abounding with blossoms of almost unimaginable variety. But in fact, this colorful oasis of stunning diversity is much more. It is one of the workhorses of Lotusland and a driving force behind its sustainable horticulture program. Recognized for its pioneering efforts to be one of the very first botanic gardens in the United States to employ environmentally responsible gardening practices, Lotusland's Insectary Garden has been crucial to this remarkable achievement and serves as a living laboratory.

This garden was originally an area where Madame Walska grew flowers for cutting and it was later referred to as the Butterfly Garden, which was a bit of a misnomer (although almost two dozen species have been recorded at the garden). As the garden has evolved, it has taken on the name Insectary Garden to recognize the beneficial coexistence of insects and plants, pollinators and predators, that contribute to its vitality and balance.

Planting a garden to increase, rather than decrease, the number of insects it attracts may seem counterintuitive, but that is precisely the strategy at work in the Insectary Garden. Planted with carefully chosen specimens that flower throughout the year, the garden becomes a magnet for beneficial predatory insects that destroy damaging pests. An example is the tiny aphid wasp (*Aphidius* spp.), which feeds on aphids, beetle larvae, leaf miners, flies, and sawflies, among others.

A diversity of flowers is also required to charm all types of useful insect allies to the garden: most plants produce flowers that are inaccessible to most insects, because their mouths are shorter than the more common pollinators, bees and butterflies. To remedy this, specimens with nectar-producing flowers with shorter tubes, such as mint, cabbage, and sunflowers are planted for their utility as well as their beauty. The delicate balance at play at all times in the Insectary Garden is just one more fascinating example of the myriad ecosystems found at Lotusland.

OPPOSITE: Oriental poppies (*Papaver orientale*) are herbaceous clump-forming plants) with crepe paper-like petals. **OVERLEAF**: The Insectary Garden was designed by Eric Nagelmann and Lotusland's Plant Health Coordinator Corey Welles, and has become an important teaching garden for Lotusland, highlighting the importance of companion planting, as well as attracting insects, and pollinators. Fifty percent of the plants in this garden are California natives; the other half are from similar climates around the world. The aviary is an homage to Madame Walska's love of birds.
PAGE 262: The dawn redwood (*Metasequoia glyptostroboides*) serves as a stately backdrop. Unlike most redwoods, the species is deciduous, so it loses its foliage in the winter. The whimsical stone structure is a fairy house. **PAGE 263**: *Bidens* 'Madame Ganna Walska' is an herbaceous perennial that was cultivated from a plant found on the estate and named in Madame's honor.

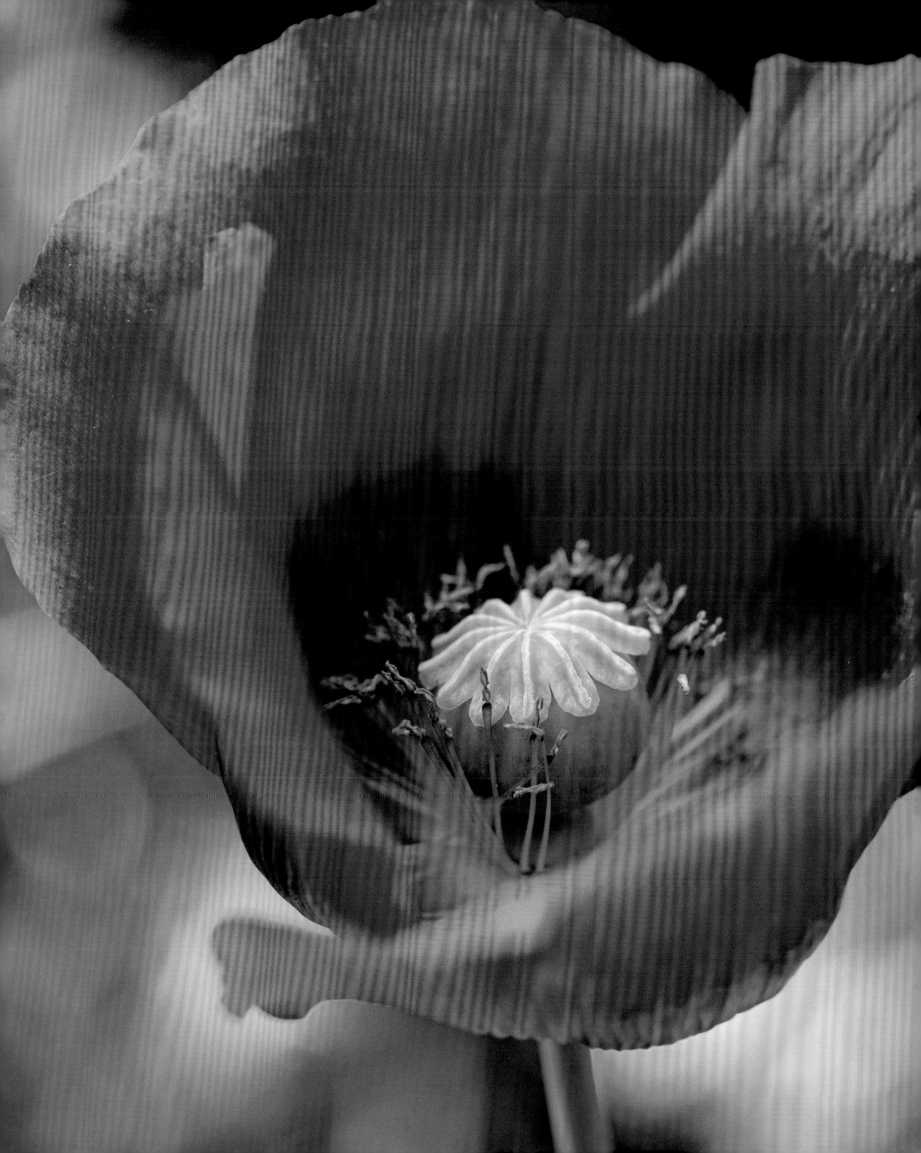

FERN GARDEN

With their delicate simplicity and stunning variety of form, few plants inspire amateur gardeners and professional horticulturalists to pursue their cultivation with such fervor as do ferns. They have been growing at Lotusland for as long as any other type of plant. Original owner Ralph Kinton Stevens planted the first ferns after making an expedition to Hawaii in 1891 to obtain specimens of the ama'u tree fern (*Sadleria cyatheoides*) for Golden Gate Park in San Francisco. Although most ended up going north, a few remained in Santa Barbara.

Unlike most plants, ferns do not flower or produce fruit, and like the unrelated mushroom, they produce spores—which grow on the underside of their fronds—rather than seeds to propagate. At Lotusland, there are airy, graceful, and light forms, but also creeping ferns that grow as ground covers (*Arthropteris tenella*), epiphytic ferns that cling to trees (staghorn fern [*Platycerium bifurcatum*]), even lithophytic ferns that can grow on rocks (holly fern [*Cyrtomium falcatum*]).

The Fern Garden at Lotusland was first created between 1968 and 1972 and was designed by horticulturalist and garden designer and fern and bromeliad expert Bill Paylen; it was doubled in size in 1987. In keeping with Madame Walska's taste and sensibility, this Fern Garden is perhaps a bit more vivacious than the subdued woodland concept that typifies many fern gardens. Paylen planted a forest of tree ferns (*Cyathea cooperi* and *Dicksonia antarctica*) that shade large swaths of chain ferns (*Woodwardia fimbriata*) and hammock ferns (*Blechnum appendiculatum*). While ferns lead the cast in this fantastic production, begonias play a key supporting role. Paylen felt the flowering plants would add contrast and color to the unrelenting green of the Fern Garden, but Madame Walska insisted she did not like begonias. "Madame, you will like them," he is reported to have said; when the garden was finished, she acknowledged that he was, indeed, correct.

OPPOSITE: *Blechnum appendiculatum*. **OVERLEAF**: Whimsical clipped eugenia topiaries add a fairy-tale-like quality to one of the Fern Garden's entrances. **PAGE 268**: Trunk detail of an Australian tree fern (*Cyathea cooperi*). **PAGE 269**: Underneath a canopy of various ferns, which thrive under the shade of coast live oaks (*Quercus agrifolia*).

With their delicate
simplicity and stunning
variety of form,
few plants inspire
amateur gardeners
and professional
horticulturalists to pursue
their cultivation with
such fervor as do ferns.

OPPOSITE: European chain ferns (*Woodwardia radicans*), with copper-colored emergent foliage. OVERLEAF: A massive staghorn fern (*Platycerium bifurcatum*, at right) is suspended from the branch of a coast live oak (*Quercus agrifolia*). PAGE 274: The fiddlehead of an Hawaiian tree fern (*Cibotium glaucum*). PAGE 275: A Tasmanian tree fern (*Dicksonia antarctica*) is surrounded by begonias and baby's tears (*Soleirolia soleirolii*) groundcover.

The Fern Garden's understory plants feature striking, yet subtle, variations of foliage and flowers, particularly begonias. **ABOVE**: Elephant's ear (*Alocasia odora*) leaf and fruit. **OPPOSITE, CLOCKWISE, FROM TOP LEFT**: The rugose foliage of *Begonia gehrtii*. The dainty flowers of *Begonia* 'Lotusland'. *Begonia* 'Lotusland' features large leaves up to ten inches in width. A cluster of begonia flowers.

"One not need be in California long before he feels his soul beginning to stir. The air is magnetized ... the consciousness awakens ... the soul must speak."

—Madame Ganna Walska

OPPOSITE: Blood Lily (*Scadoxus multiflorus* ssp. *katharinae*), seen here, is native to South Africa.

AFTERWORD

Madame Ganna Walska's vision created Lotusland. Its legacy owes a great debt to many others who have shared in her unique vision. Hania P. Tallmadge, Ganna Walska's niece, today continues the family connection and commitment.

Decades of volunteers have since shaped and served Lotusland. Many devoted trustees have guided and supported the organization, and countless docents and community volunteers, gardeners, and staff have applied their talents to care for the garden and foster the values it represents.

Lotusland is also dependent on the donors whose generosity sustains the garden. Despite the challenges in operating with the attendance limitations and operational restrictions imposed by its County of Santa Barbara Conditional Use Permit, Lotusland is preserved and enhanced thanks to the investment of loyal individuals and foundations.

While the garden's living collections are mature and magnificent, as an institution Lotusland is young compared to other world-class gardens, a garden full of innovation and fresh ideas inhabiting important historic buildings and grounds. Lotusland's mission continues to evolve, responding to the conditions of the day, including conserving plant species that are threatened or extinct in the wild, combating climate change through environmental management, and regenerative horticultural practices that represent the best in scientific and responsible living collections stewardship.

Those who are just beginning the journey to discover Lotusland should visit this extraordinary botanical nirvana. When you do, please consider participating in the Garden's growth and advancement to ensure that our children, and future generations, may experience its wonder.

OPPOSITE: *Catalpa speciosa.*

HIGHLIGHTS FROM
THE LIVING COLLECTIONS

Lotusland is home to more than 3,400 types of plants, including at least 35,000 specimens. Many species of plants at the gardens are threatened in nature and are restricted from wild collection and international trade. To learn more about individual plants in the living collections, visit lotusland.org, where every specimen can be searched for by species or plant family. The website is also a real-time resource for information on Lotusland's ever-developing plant conservation initiatives and recent partnerships with other botanic organizations, as well as the latest updates on its green garden strategies. On these pages are seventy-five unusual or important specimens that, when combined with Lotusland's flair for mass plantings and eccentric juxtapositions, give the garden its unmistakable, idiosyncratic style.

Aloe marlothii hybrid

Nymphaea 'Madame Ganna Walska'

Agave gypsophila

Brahea aculeata

Butia capitata

Lemna minor and dried lotus pods

Aloe salm-dyckiana

Aloe confusa

Aloe lutescens

Pachycereus pringlei and *Echinocactus grusonii* (foreground)

Nymphaea 'Clyde Ikins'

Catalpa speciosa

Acer palmatum

Phyllostachys bambusoides

Ajuga reptans 'Black Scallop'

Euphorbia resinifera

Euphorbia ammak
'Variegata'

Euphorbia clandestina

Dudleya brittonii

Chamaedorea microspadix

Oreocereus celsianus

Bismarckia nobilis

Nelumbo nucifera

Nymphaea 'Wanvisa'

Scadoxus multiflorus
ssp. katharinae

Selenicereus hamatus

Ficus carica 'Panache'

Alocasia odora

Aloe elgonica

Aloe marlothii

Xanthorrhoea preissii

Callistemon 'Cane's Hybrid'

Citrus junos

Prunus persica 'Red Baron'

Hakea petiolaris

Brachychiton acerifolius

Pilosocereus species

Monstera deliciosa

Echinopsis spachiana

Echinopsis huascha

Encephalartos lanatus

Pseudobombax ellipticum

Encephalartos latifrons

Cycas revoluta

Dioon oaxacensis

Encephalartos
friderici-guilielmi

Aeonium
arboreum 'Zwartkop'

Citrus medica var.
sarcodactylis

Echeveria elegans

Alluaudia procera

Neoregelia carolinae

Aechmea 'Del Mar'

Aechmea gamosepala

Begonia 'Lotusland'

Billbergia

284

Citrus limon 'Pink Lemonade'

Papaver orientale

Bidens 'Madame Ganna Walska'

Encephalartos ferox

Lepidozamia peroffskyana

Blechnum appendiculatum

Ceratozamia latifolia

Encephalartos heenanii

Cyathea cooperi

Ceratozamia fuscoviridis

Woodwardia radicans

Oscularia deltoides

Dicksonia antarctica

Agave franzosinii

Beaucarnea recurvata

Vriesea platynema

Cibotium glaucum

Armatocereus mataranus

Begonia gehrtii

Opuntia galapageia var. profusa

285

ACKNOWLEDGMENTS

We are extremely grateful to the myriad of people who helped bring this book to fruition: Curator Paul Mills and Historian Rose Thomas for their invaluable insight and knowledge on all things Lotusland; Jeff Chemnick, Mike Furner, Arthur Gaudi, Eric Nagelmann, Hania Tallmadge, and Corey Welles for sharing their observations garnered over many years; and Rebecca Anderson, our Executive Director, for her help wherever and whenever needed.

Trustees Marc Appleton, Dorothy Gardner, Suzanne Mathews and Alexandra Morse formed the committee which inspired the book's creation and guided its development through to publication.

We are indebted to Doug Turshen for his elegant book design, to Clinton Smith and to Jill Cohen Associates LLC for their substantial contributions. We owe a special acknowledgement to our photographer Lisa Romerein, and her assistant, Dean Courtois, whose images capture the magic of the garden and bring it to life.

Our thanks to publisher Charles Miers and to our editor, Douglas Curran, at Rizzoli U. S. A., whose enthusiastic commitment never wavered from the moment they came onboard.

Finally, this book happened because of the generosity of our patrons, who took a leap of faith when it was still just an idea:

Marc Appleton
Sharon and David Bradford
Dorothy and John Gardner
Elisabeth Morse Giovine
Belle Hahn
Joan and Palmer Jackson Sr.
Suzanne and Gilbert Mathews
Alexandra and Charles Morse
Guillermo Nicolas and Jim Foster
Cynthia and Chapin Nolen
Connie and John Pearcy
Lynda Weinman and Bruce Heavin

First published in the United States of America in 2022 by
RIZZOLI INTERNATIONAL PUBLICATIONS, INC.
300 Park Avenue South, New York, NY 10010
www.rizzoliusa.com

In association with
GANNA WALSKA LOTUSLAND
695 Ashley Road, Santa Barbara, CA 93108
www.lotusland.org

Foreword: Marc Appleton
Photography (except as indicated below): Lisa Romerein
Photographs on pages 13, 172, 244, 250: J. R. Eyerman,
Ganna Walska Lotusland Archives
Photograph on page 64: Couresty Ganna Walska Lotusland Archives
Edited by the board and staff of Lotusland and written with the
assistance of Clinton Smith

Publisher: Charles Miers
Editor: Douglas Curran
Production Manager: Kaija Markoe
Managing Editor: Lynn Scrabis
Developed in conjunction with Jill Cohen Associates, LLC.

Designed by Doug Turshen with David Huang

Printed and bound in China

2022 2023 2024 2025 2026/ 10 9 8 7 6 5 4 3 2 1

ISBN-13: 978-0-8478-6989-3
Library of Congress Control Number: 2021945301

Visit us online:
Facebook.com/RizzoliNewYork
Twitter: @Rizzoli_Books
Instagram.com/RizzoliBooks
Pinterest.com/RizzoliBooks
Youtube.com/user/RizzoliNY
Issuu.com/Rizzoli